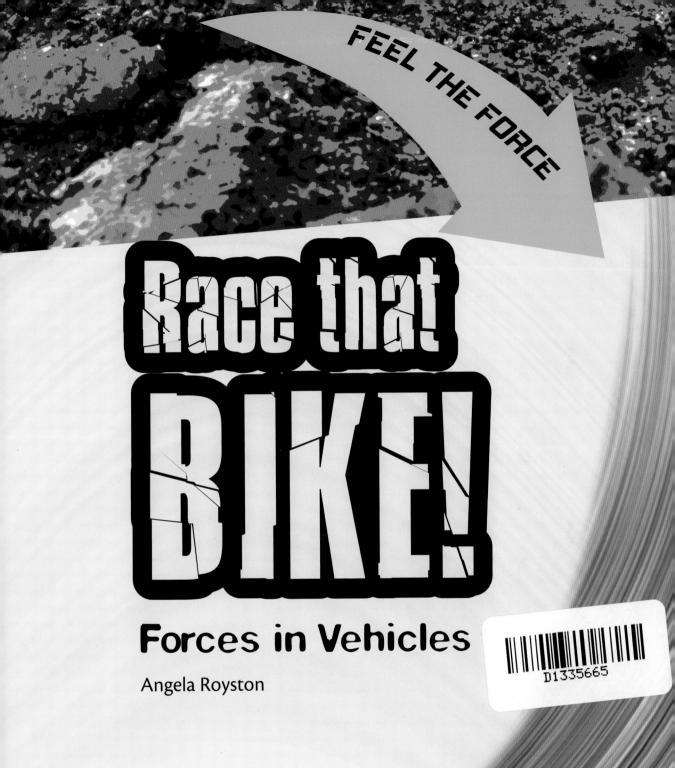

Race that BIKE!

Forces in Vehicles

Angela Royston

raintree

Raintree is an imprint of Capstone Global Library Limited, a company incorporated in England and Wales having its registered office at 7 Pilgrim Street, London, EC4V 6LB – Registered company number: 6695582

www.raintree.co.uk
myorders@raintree.co.uk

Edited by Helen Cox Cannons and Holly Beaumont
Designed by Philippa Jenkins
Original illustrations © Capstone Global Library Ltd 2015
Illustrated by HL Studios, Witney, Oxon
Picture research by Tracy Cummins
Production by Helen McCreath
Originated by Capstone Global Library Ltd
Printed and Bound in China by Leo Paper Group

ISBN 978 1 406 29648 8 (hardback)
19 18 17 16 15
10 9 8 7 6 5 4 3 2 1

ISBN 978 1 406 29653 2 (paperback)
20 19 18 17 16
10 9 8 7 6 5 4 3 2 1

British Library Cataloguing in Publication Data
A full catalogue record for this book is available from the British Library.

Acknowledgements
We would like to thank the following for permission to reproduce photographs: Capstone Press: HL Studios, 9, 11, 19, Karon Dubke, 14, 15, 26, 27, 36, 37; Dreamstime: Jorg Hackemann, 7; Getty Images: China Photos, 25, Granger Wootz, 6, Grant Faint, 31, Keystone-France, 8; Science Source: GIPhotoStock, 29; Shutterstock: Amy Walters, 18, B747, 34, connel, 12, dibrova, 21, Digital Media Pro, 35, 43 Bottom, Dudarev Mikhail, 28, Helmut Spoonwood, 38, i4lcocl2, 23, 43 Middle, Ike L, 4, Ljupco Smokovski, Front Cover, Maksim Toome, 40, optimarc, 39, Pawel Nawrot, 13, Radu Razvan, 17, 42 Top, Rock and Wasp, 30, Steve Cordory, 10, 42 Bottom, Tina Jeans, 22, Vadim Ratnikov, Design Element, wiktord, 41, Yongcharoen_kittiyaporn, 5, Zdorov Kirill Vladimirovich, 33; Thinkstock: GYRO PHOTOGRAPHY/amana imagesRF, 20, 43 Top.

We would like to thank Patrick O'Mahony for his invaluable help in the preparation of this book.

Every effort has been made to contact copyright holders of material reproduced in this book. Any omissions will be rectified in subsequent printings if notice is given to the publisher.

Contents

Some words are shown in bold, **like this**. You can find out what they mean by looking in the glossary.

What makes a vehicle move?

In a velodrome, cyclists race around the sloped side of the track. The winner is the rider who can cycle fastest at just the right moment.

A force is needed to make anything, including a vehicle, move. Vehicles are special because they allow us to move faster than we can on our own. With bicycles and scooters, our muscles provide the force to move them, while the engines in aircraft, cars and other vehicles produce much stronger forces. Different kinds of forces affect a vehicle as it moves.

WHEELS

Wheels allow a land vehicle to move more easily than sliding it across the ground. A wheel reduces the area in contact with the ground, but, more importantly, a wheel increases the effect of a force. Using a small force to turn the **hub** of a wheel makes the rim of the wheel travel a much greater distance.

Hub -----
Rim -----
Tyre -----

Increasing the speed

To win a race, you have to go faster than everyone else. A moving vehicle will keep going at a steady speed as long as the forces acting on it remain balanced. To accelerate and go faster, the force producing the movement has to be increased or the force pushing against the movement decreased. Different forces are applied to slow down and stop the vehicle when the race is over.

This chunky tyre is good for racing over rough ground.

Steering

You need to steer so that you can turn corners and avoid hitting other vehicles and obstacles. To steer a vehicle, the rider or driver has to turn the front wheel or wheels. Turning the handlebars of a bicycle turns the front wheel. In a car, a steering wheel is connected to the front wheels to change direction.

Why is a scooter easy to ride?

A kick scooter is one of the simplest vehicles. It consists of a footboard or deck, a handlebar and wheels. Children as young as three years old can ride a scooter, but older children and adults also use them to get about and for fun.

Push and glide

It is easy to ride a scooter. With one foot on the deck, you push against the ground with your other foot. As the scooter rolls forward, the rider brings the pushing leg on to the deck, ready to push again. The handlebar helps the rider to balance on one leg as the other leg pushes. The handlebar connects directly to the front wheel so that steering is very quick and accurate.

Most scooters have two wheels, but scooters for young children often have three or four wheels so that it is easier for the child to balance.

A kick scooter is like a skateboard with a handlebar. After lots of practice, riders can perform tricks such as jumps, fast turns and somersaults.

Slowing down and stopping

The simplest scooters do not have brakes. When the scooter is moving quite slowly, the rider drags their foot along the ground so that a force called **friction** stops the movement. Scooters may have brakes, which also use friction to slow the scooter down. The rider uses one foot to press down on a piece of metal over the back wheel. When the metal touches the wheel, friction comes into play to stop the scooter.

Why can bicycles go faster than scooters?

Bicycles and scooters both have two wheels, but a bicycle can go much faster than a scooter, and a cyclist can keep going for much longer. The main differences between them are the size of the wheels and the pedals. A bicycle has much bigger wheels than a scooter. Bigger wheels take more effort to turn, especially uphill, but the pedals reduce the amount of effort needed to cycle.

Big or small wheels?

Small wheels are easier to control, but they cover less distance with each turn. Every time a scooter wheel turns, the scooter moves forwards by about 30 centimetres (12 inches). However, every time a bicycle wheel turns, the bike moves forwards by about 2 metres (7 feet). This means that the scooter's wheels have to turn nearly seven times to cover the same distance as one turn of the bicycle wheel. Without pedals, turning a bicycle wheel would quickly become tiring.

Penny-farthing bicycles were popular in the 1870s and 1880s. The pedals were fixed directly to the large front wheel, which made cycling hard work!

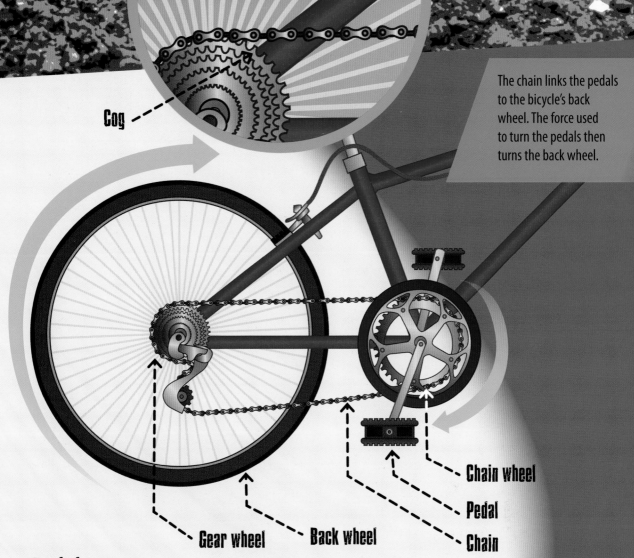

Cog

The chain links the pedals to the bicycle's back wheel. The force used to turn the pedals then turns the back wheel.

Chain wheel

Pedal

Chain

Gear wheel

Back wheel

Pedal power

The pedals are connected to the back wheel by a chain, which transmits the movement of the pedals to the back wheel. To do this, the pedals are joined to the **chain wheel**, which turns as the pedals turn. The chain wheel has **cogs**, or teeth, which fit into the links of the chain.

Turning the back wheel

The chain also fits around the cogs of the **gear wheel** so that, as the chain wheel rotates, the chain turns the gear wheel. The gear wheel is fixed to the hub of the back wheel and so moves the bicycle forwards. The gear wheel is usually smaller than the chain wheel, so it and the back wheel rotate faster than the pedals.

Efficient vehicles

Bicycles are one of the most efficient vehicles. You waste very little energy as you use your muscles to cycle. A bicycle is carefully designed to give maximum speed for least effort, and **gears** help the rider adjust to different situations.

Lightweight

Bicycles are designed to be lightweight. The wheels have **spokes**, which make them strong but not heavy. A solid wheel would take much more effort to turn. The bicycle frame is made of lightweight metal. This means that your effort goes into moving you, the rider, not the bike.

Changing gear

Gears allow you to adjust the amount of energy and force you use to pedal. If you are cycling uphill, you can change to a gear that makes pedalling easier, but moves the bicycle more slowly. If you are speeding along the flat, a higher gear increases the number of times the back wheel turns for every turn of the pedals.

Each cogged wheel is a different gear. The smaller wheels give the higher gears.

The cogs lock together so that when one wheel turns, it forces the other wheel to turn in the opposite direction. Smaller wheels have fewer cogs, which means they go faster and rotate more often than the bigger wheels.

HOW GEARS WORK

A bicycle with gears has several gear wheels that are different sizes. This allows the rider to choose how fast the back wheel moves compared to the chain wheel and pedals. Most bikes have between three and nine toothed gear wheels. When the rider changes gear, he or she moves the chain from one gear wheel to another. The larger gear wheels make the back wheel turn more slowly and so the rider uses them to go uphill. The smaller gear wheels make the back wheel turn faster, and so he or she uses them to increase speed.

Why do tyres have treads?

Road vehicles, including bicycles, cars, lorries and buses, have wheels covered with tough rubber **tyres**. The tyres are filled with air and the rubber has a raised pattern moulded into it, called the **tread**. These tyres give more grip on wet surfaces and are safer than tyres without treads would be.

Cushioning the bumps

Early bicycles had hard steel wheels and were called bone shakers because the rider felt every bump in the untarred and pot-holed roads. Today's **pneumatic** tyres, which are made of rubber and filled with air, were invented in 1888. The part of the tyre in contact with the ground is **compressed**, or squashed, by the weight of the rider, and absorbs the shock of the bumps in an uneven road.

Gripping the road

Friction helps tyres to grip the road. Friction is created when one surface moves across or rubs against another surface, and its effect is to slow a vehicle down. The amount of friction depends on the materials in contact and how rough or smooth they are. Rough surfaces create more friction.

The weight of the cyclist compresses the part of the tyre in contact with the road. This allows more of the treads to grip the road.

Off-road vehicles have wide tyres with deep treads. The width of the tyres increases the area in contact with the ground, and the tread increases the grip so the wheels are less likely to slip.

Skidding

Treads make the vehicle less likely to slide or **skid**. This is useful when going round bends and on slippery surfaces. Tractors and off-road cars and bikes have deep treads to help them grip on soft or muddy ground. Racing cars are fitted with smooth tyres when the racetrack is dry. Wet surfaces, however, are more slippery than dry ones, so the tyres are changed to ones with treads if it rains.

ACTIVITY: Measuring friction

It's time to ramp it up with this experiment, as you compare the force of friction produced by different materials. Explore how rough surfaces compare with smooth ones and find out which material will allow a toy car to travel the furthest.

You will need:
- a flat board about 50 cm (20 in.) long and 15 cm (6 in.) wide
- different surfaces, such as metal foil, rough sandpaper, sugar paper, shiny
- wrapping paper
- a smooth floor
- masking tape
- several books
- a toy car
- a measuring tape
- paper and pencil

1 Make a pile of books about 10 cm (4 in.) high on the floor. Cover the board with metal foil, using masking tape to hold the foil in place.

2 Lean the board against the books. Mark where the board touches the books. Make sure there is room in front of the board for the car to roll.

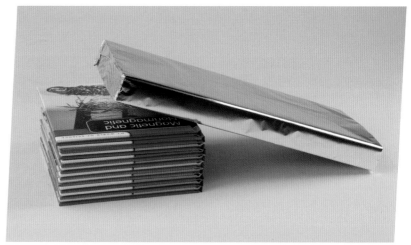

3 Place the car on the slope so that its back wheels are at the very top of the board. Always start the car from the same place when you repeat the test.

4 Let the car go and mark where it stops. Measure the distance from the mark to the bottom of the board.

5 Replace the metal foil with another material. Lean the board against the books using the marks you made in step 2. Repeat the test.

6 Repeat with each material. Which surface has most friction? Which has least?

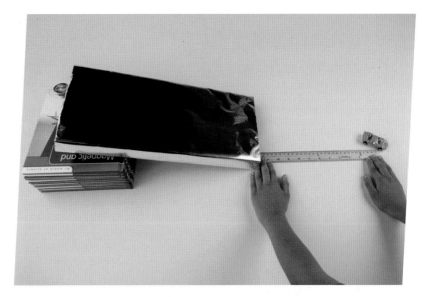

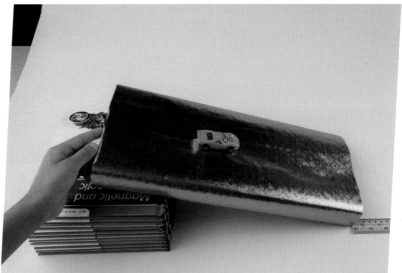

Conclusion

You should have found that the car travelled furthest after rolling down the smoothest materials. Smooth surfaces produce less friction and so allow the car to travel faster. The faster the speed the further the car rolls, until friction slows the car to a halt.

How does a bike's design increase speed?

Designers and engineers increase speed by reducing the forces that slow down movement – particularly friction and **air resistance**. Friction is produced between the tyres and the road, and increases with weight, so racing bikes are made of lightweight materials. Air resistance pushes back against any surface moving through the air.

AIR RESISTANCE

It is a law of physics that when a force pushes against something, that thing then pushes back with an opposing force. As a moving vehicle forces its way through the air, the air pushes back with an opposing force, called air resistance. The larger the area pushing against the air, the greater the force resisting it.

Streamlined racers

Wide, flat shapes create the most air resistance, while narrow, pointed shapes reduce air resistance. A **streamlined** shape cuts through the air and allows the air to flow smoothly round it. Racing bicycles are designed with low, narrow handlebars so that the rider bends forward to grip them. To increase the streamlining, cycle helmets curve smoothly around the head.

Racing tyres

Cyclists use different tyres for different tracks. A hard material produces less friction, but is more likely to slip than a softer one. A narrow tyre is more streamlined than a broader tyre, but is more likely to sink into the ground if used off a hard road. The result is that racing bikes usually have larger wheels with narrow, hard tyres. Off-road bikes have smaller wheels with broad tyres and deep treads.

The Tour de France is the biggest cycle race in the world. Cyclists from many countries compete over three weeks and cover about 3,600 kilometres (2,235 miles).

Streamlined helmet

Shoes with treads to grip pedals

direction of wheel rotation

direction of wheel rotation

How does a car engine work?

Nearly all cars use the same type of engine – the **internal combustion engine**. This burns fuel and uses the energy released to create movement that is transmitted from the engine to the wheels.

Inside the engine

An internal combustion engine has several cylinders, each with a **piston** that moves up and down to take in fuel and air, burn the fuel, and push out the waste gases. The pistons are attached to a **crankshaft**, which changes the up–down movement of the pistons to a turning movement. The rotating crankshaft is joined to an **axle**, which turns the back wheel of a motorbike and the front or back wheels of a car.

Waste gases escape from the engine into the air through exhaust pipes.

Problems with petrol engines

The fact that internal combustion engines burn petrol or diesel oil means that their **exhaust gases** contain **carbon dioxide** and other **greenhouse gases**. Greenhouse gases cause global warming and **climate change**, which threatens Earth's survival. Other ways of powering vehicles are being developed that use the energy of electricity to produce movement.

FOUR-STROKE CYLINDER

A cylinder goes through four stages over and over again to turn fuel into movement that turns the crankshaft.

INTERNAL COMBUSTION ENGINE

Air and fuel fed in

1. INDUCTION
A small amount of fuel and air is fed into the top of the cylinder.

Fuel and air squashed

2. COMPRESSION
The piston moves up and compresses, or squashes, the fuel and air.

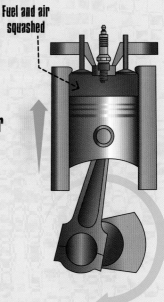

Combustion (explosion) caused by spark. Fuel is lit.

3. POWER
The fuel is lit by an electric spark and explodes.

Cylinder pushed down. Waste gases drawn out of top of cylinder.

4. EXHAUST
The force of the explosion pushes the cylinder down and the waste gases are drawn out of the top of the cylinder.

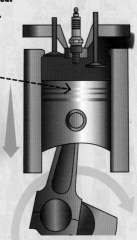

These four stages bring the cylinder back to the start of the cycle.

What makes a suspension bridge special?

Bridges and tunnels help to make road and rail journeys shorter. Many of the world's most famous bridges, including the Golden Gate Bridge in San Francisco, U.S.A and the Humber Bridge in the UK, are **suspension bridges**. Suspension bridges have a long main **span**, so they are often used to cross gorges, rivers and other stretches of water.

Suspended from a cable

A suspension bridge consists of two massive steel **cables**, each slung over two tall towers. The cables are anchored in deep concrete or solid rock at each end of the bridge. The road or railway is laid on top of beams, which are attached to thinner cables called hangers and hung from the main overhead cables.

Longer spans

Engineers have been building bridges with longer and longer spans. The longest suspension bridge in the world is the Akashi-Kaikyo in Japan. Its main span is 1,991 metres (6,532 feet) long and it links the island of Awaji to the city of Kobe on the main island of Honshu.

The Akashi-Kaikyo suspension bridge in Japan is the longest in the world. It is designed to be strong enough to withstand severe earthquakes, hurricane winds and fast sea currents.

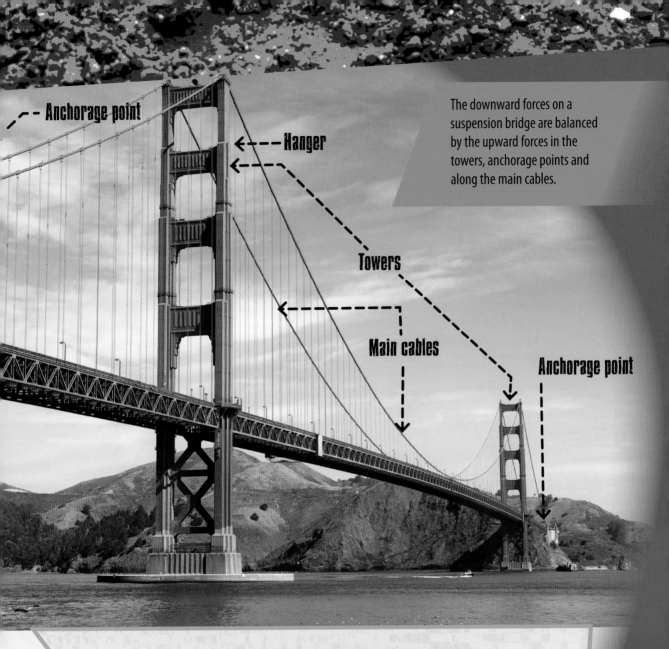

Anchorage point

Hanger

The downward forces on a suspension bridge are balanced by the upward forces in the towers, anchorage points and along the main cables.

Towers

Main cables

Anchorage point

FOLLOW THE FORCES

The weight of vehicles presses down on the beams and is counteracted by an upward force to the towers. The hangers pull down on the main cable, but these forces are offset along the cable to the top of each tower and the anchorage points. The cable pulls down on the towers and the anchorage points, which support the weight of the cable by pushing upwards with an equal force.

Do rails help trains go faster?

Trains have many smooth wheels and run on smooth rails, so friction between the wheels and rails is much less than between tyres and road surfaces. Although trains are much bigger than cars, the low friction allows them to reach higher speeds. Friction is so low that freight trains can carry massive loads.

Smooth wheels

Rails and train wheels are both made of steel, because steel is hardwearing, keeps its shape and produces little friction. The wheels have a **flange** on the inner side so that they cannot slide off the rails. Friction between the wheels and rails is incredibly low. This means that the wheels do not have enough grip for the train to accelerate and brake quickly. Engineers have overcome this problem by automatically spraying each wheel with sand when the train needs extra grip.

Flange stops wheel slipping off the rail

Smooth surfaces

The weight of a train is spread over many wheels. This reduces friction for each wheel and spreads the weight along the rail.

The heaviest freight trains use two locomotives, one at the front and one at the back, to give them extra power.

Providing the driving force

A locomotive is the engine that powers the train. Some locomotives burn diesel fuel, while others have electric motors. An electric motor takes electricity either from an overhead wire, or from an electrified third rail. Diesel engines are more powerful and are used to drive long freight trains, whose enormous weight is shared between all the wheels of the many wagons.

High-speed trains

The fastest trains carry passengers, and they are driven by electric motors. High-speed electric trains carry people between cities in Europe and in Asia. The locomotives at the front of the train are streamlined to reduce air resistance. They are much faster than cars and produce much less greenhouse gas per passenger than aeroplanes or cars over the same distance.

What is the fastest train?

The world's fastest trains have no engine and usually no wheels! These trains use the force of **magnetism** to drive them. They are called maglev trains, which is short for magnetic levitation. The moving train avoids any friction between the train and the rails because the surfaces are not touching.

How maglev works

Two magnets may attract or repel each other. Maglev uses the force of repulsion to lift, drive and guide the train. When an electric current passes through a coil of wire wound around an iron core, it creates an **electromagnet**. The train has electromagnets under it and along the sides of the track. The magnets repel each other, causing the train to lift off the track. The flow of electricity is then controlled to produce a force that pushes the train forwards.

MAGNETIC POLES

The two ends of a magnet are called the poles. One is the north pole (N) and the other is the south pole (S). If you bring the north pole of one magnet towards the south pole of another, the two magnets will be drawn together. If, however, you bring two north poles (or two south poles) together, the magnets will push each other apart.

Like poles repel

Different poles attract

A maglev train floats just above the track in Shanghai. The greatest force stopping a maglev train going faster is air resistance.

The fastest train

Maglev trains can go faster than electric high-speed trains. In Shanghai, China, a maglev train speeds passengers from the city to the airport 31 kilometres (19 miles) away. Travelling at 430 kilometres (267 miles) per hour, the journey takes only about 8 minutes. Several countries are developing even faster maglev trains.

ACTIVITY: Floating magnets

See how maglev trains work by getting magnets to hover one above the other. This experiment uses ring magnets in which the poles are the opposite sides of the ring.

You will need:
- three ring magnets
- a piece of modelling clay
- a pencil

1 Play with the magnets. Can you get them to attract each other and repel each other? Place two magnets with like poles together on the table. What happens?

2 Stick the pencil in the clay and put one of the magnets over it.

3 Take a second magnet and put it over the first. If the magnets stick together then turn the top magnet over. What happens?

4 Add the third magnet. Which pole should you put face to face with the one below it so that they repel each other? Try it. Were you right?

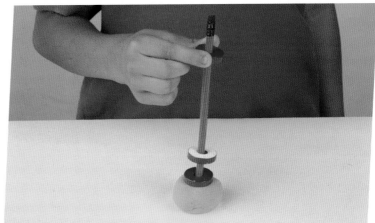

Conclusion

When you put two like poles together, the magnets slide sideways. When you put them over the pencil firmly fixed into the modelling clay, the pencil stops them sliding to the side. Instead, the top one floats above the lower one. This is how a maglev train floats above the track. Adding a third magnet shows that the force of repulsion from the second magnet is greater than the force of attraction to the lowest magnet. This is because magnetic force decreases with distance.

27

How do boats float?

Large boats are made of steel and other heavy materials, so why do they float? The answer is that a boat is filled with air, and this makes it light for its size. If a boat fills with water, it is no longer light for its size and it sinks. A boat has several forces working on it, including **gravity** and **upthrust**, the force that keeps it afloat.

Two forces determine whether a boat floats or sinks. Upthrust pushes upwards against gravity, whose downward pull depends on the weight of the boat. The boat floats when the two forces are balanced.

gravity

upthrust

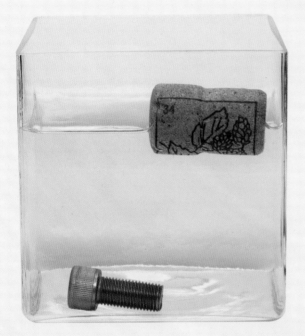

DENSITY AND UPTHRUST

The weight of an object compared to its size is called **density**. A small, heavy object, such as a stone, is denser than a large, light object, such as a balloon. When an object is put into water, it pushes aside an amount of water. The displaced water creates a force that pushes back, called upthrust. If the upthrust balances the force of gravity, the object floats. If it is less than gravity, the object sinks.

This cork floats because it is less dense than water. The metal bolt sinks because it is more dense than water.

Staying afloat

Gravity pulls all objects, including boats, towards the centre of Earth. The weight of an object is a measure of the force of gravity. An object that is lighter than the same volume of water is said to be **buoyant**, which means that it can easily float. Large boats trap a huge volume of air inside them and this makes the boat buoyant. Rafts and surfboards are made of lightweight materials. They are light enough for the water to support their weight when it is spread over a large area.

What drives boats?

People have invented many different ways to push a boat through water. Even today, some boats use sails and oars, as explorers and traders did for more than 2,000 years. However, most ships and boats are driven by propellers, which are turned by the ship's engines.

To paddle a canoe, you force the blade of the paddle backwards through the water. The water pushes back, forcing the canoe forwards.

Hand pushes handle forwards

Paddle pivots

Blade pushes water backwards

Paddling your own canoe

Paddles push the water backwards to move the canoe forwards. The paddle is a **lever**, a simple machine that can change a push into a pull. As one arm pushes the handle of the paddle forwards, the paddle **pivots**, or turns, around the other hand so that the blade of the paddle moves backwards through the water.

Propellers

A boat propeller connected to a motor engine pushes the water backwards to propel the boat forwards. A boat has no brakes. Instead, the propellers rotate in the opposite direction to push the water forwards. As the water pushes back, it slows the boat down.

Propeller

Rudder

This boat is driven by a spinning propeller and steered by turning the rudder.

HOW A PROPELLER WORKS

A propeller changes circular movement into forward movement. Large ships have two propellers attached to the stern under the water. As a propeller turns, its blades push the seawater backwards. The water reacts by pushing in the opposite direction to propel the boat forwards.

Steering

A **rudder** is a simple device for steering and is attached to the stern (the back of the boat) below the surface of the water. When the rudder is turned a few degrees to the right, for example, the water pushes against it and forces the stern to the left. This brings the bow (the front of the boat) around to the right.

Speedboats

A speedboat has a powerful engine, but increasing the power of the engine is not the only way to increase the speed. If the engine is too powerful, the boat becomes hard to control and can even take off into the air. Speedboats move fast because they are designed to reduce the main force that slows them down – **water resistance**.

Water resistance

Water resistance acts like air resistance (see page 16). As an object moves through the water, the water pushes back. The greater the area of the surface pushing through the water, the greater the force of water resistance. Boat designers use streamlining to reduce the area that punches against the water.

Streamlining

Most boats narrow to a point at the front so that the bow can cut through the water. The water then flows smoothly on either side of the boat. The body of the boat (the hull) also curves under the boat. The curve allows water to flow out from under the boat and so helps to reduce water resistance.

Skimming the waves

Water is denser than air, so water resistance is stronger than air resistance. Speedboats increase speed by lifting the front part of the boat out of the water so that it is moving through air. The bow and hull are specially shaped so that, as the boat speeds forward, the water pushes the bow upwards. The faster the boat moves, the higher the hull is pushed up. The heavy engine at the back (stern) stops the whole boat from taking off.

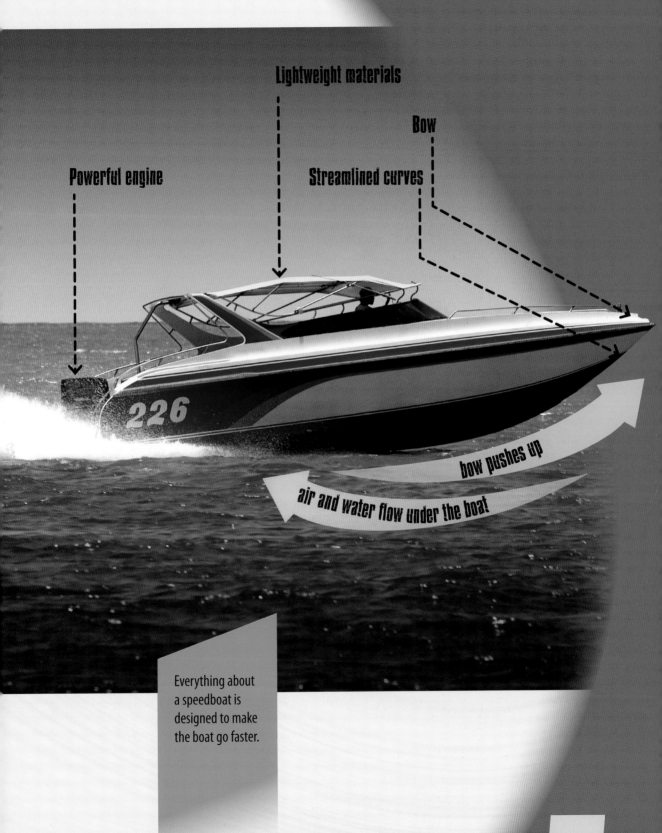

Lightweight materials

Bow

Powerful engine

Streamlined curves

bow pushes up

air and water flow under the boat

226

Everything about a speedboat is designed to make the boat go faster.

How do aircraft take off?

An aircraft speeds down the runway. When its speed is fast enough, the nose of the plane tilts upwards and the aircraft lifts up into the air. Planes have powerful engines to propel them forwards along the ground and through the air, but it is the shape of the wings that makes it possible for the aircraft to lift up and stay in the sky.

Aeroplane wings

For an aircraft to take off, it has to overcome the forces of gravity and air resistance. The shape of an aircraft's wings produces a force called **lift**, which is stronger than gravity and pushes the plane off the ground and into the air. Aeroplanes have long, wide wings that are curved on top but flat underneath. The shape of the wing diverts air downwards, creating a down force on the air. The air then reacts by creating an equal but opposite force, which pushes the wing up.

A large passenger aircraft weighs up to 560 tonnes (617 tons) as it prepares to take off. It takes a huge force to lift it into the air.

lift

lift

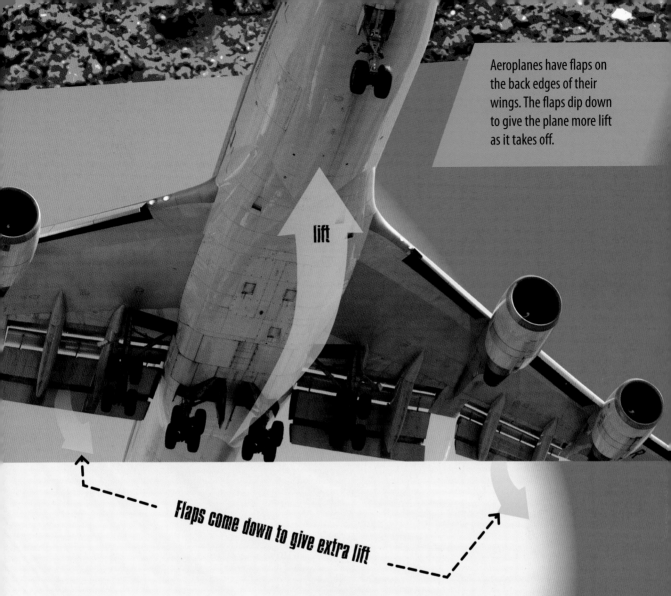

Aeroplanes have flaps on the back edges of their wings. The flaps dip down to give the plane more lift as it takes off.

lift

Flaps come down to give extra lift

Helicopters

Helicopters do not have wings. Instead, the engine turns propeller blades on top of the aircraft. As the blades turn, they produce lift. The pilot changes the angle of the blades to lift the helicopter up, move it forwards or backwards, hold it still as it hovers, or slowly let it drop back to the ground.

LIFT

The curve of an aircraft wing or helicopter blade gives it a larger surface on top than underneath. This means that air travels faster over the top of the wing than under it, and produces a smaller downward force than up force, so creating lift.

ACTIVITY: Testing air resistance

A helicopter has long blades that rotate very fast to give the vehicle lift. In this experiment, you will see how rotating blades slow down the speed at which a paper helicopter falls to the ground. By timing several paper helicopters with different length and width of blades, you can test which design gives best air resistance.

You will need:
- several sheets of A4 paper
- ruler
- a pencil
- scissors
- several paperclips
- stopwatch

1 Cut a rectangle of paper 10 x 21 cm (4 x 8 in.). Fold the rectangle lengthways down the middle.

2 Mark two small crosses on the fold line, 8 cm (3 in.) from each end. Cut down the fold to reach one of these crosses. This will form your blades.

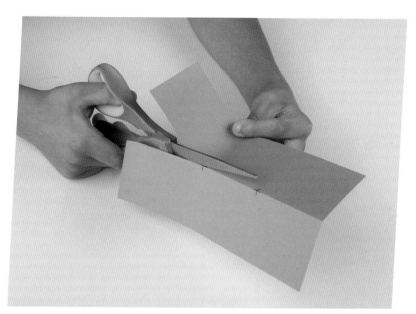

3 Keeping your paper folded, at the second cross draw a line across the narrowest width. Mark a half-way point, 2.5 cm (1 in.) along this line and cut from the open edge of the paper until you reach this point.

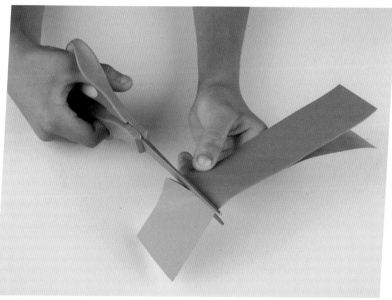

4 Unfolding the paper, fold these sections in towards the central crease and clip them in place with two paperclips. Next, fold one blade forwards and the other backwards so that both are at right angles to the rest of the helicopter.

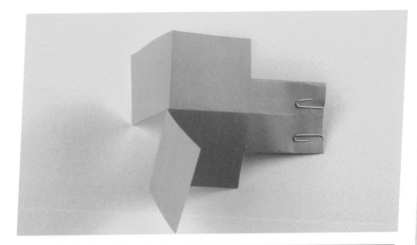

5 Drop the helicopter from as high above the floor as you can. Even better, ask an adult for help or drop it over the banisters of a staircase. Time how long it takes for the helicopter to reach the floor.

6 Make other helicopters with wider, narrower, shorter and longer wings. Which shape takes longest to drop? It has created the most lift! Notice which one spins the fastest.

Conclusion

The helicopter that took the longest time to fall should be the one with the blades that have the largest area. This could be achieved by making the blades wider or longer. The faster a helicopter spins, the more uplift it creates.

Why can't an aircraft fly into space?

Jet aircraft fly up to about 12 kilometres (7½ miles) above the ground, while a spacecraft orbits more than 200 kilometres (125 miles) above Earth. It takes a rocket and a huge amount of fuel to get a spacecraft into space, yet jet engines and rockets are very similar. The main difference is that jet engines take in **oxygen** from the air.

Flying high

The air becomes thinner the higher you are above Earth. Scientists agree that space begins at a height of about 100 kilometres (62 miles), although there is still some air here. The highest that a passenger aircraft can fly safely is less than an eighth of that. Above this height, the air is too thin for the wings to work and there is not enough oxygen in the air for the jet engines to work.

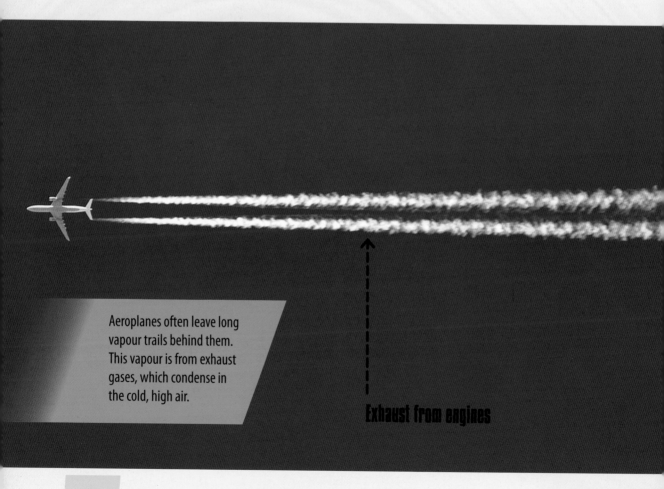

Aeroplanes often leave long vapour trails behind them. This vapour is from exhaust gases, which condense in the cold, high air.

Exhaust from engines

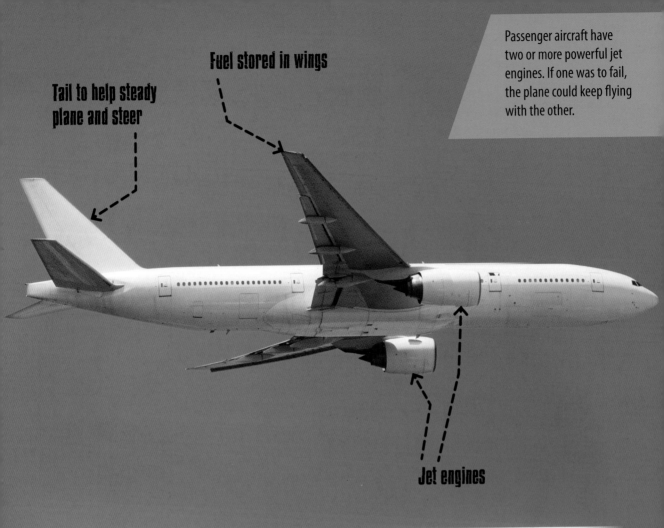

Tail to help steady plane and steer

Fuel stored in wings

Passenger aircraft have two or more powerful jet engines. If one was to fail, the plane could keep flying with the other.

Jet engines

Jet engines

A jet engine sucks in air and uses the oxygen in it to burn aviation fuel. The engine then pushes the exhaust gases backwards out of the engine at great speed. The exhaust gases push back against the air, which reacts by pushing the plane forwards. Passenger aircraft have two or four powerful jet engines to propel them through the skies.

Rocket engines

Rockets also burn fuel and force out a jet of exhaust gases under great pressure. A rocket directs the spacecraft straight up into the air and does not need wings. A rocket carries its own supply of oxygen, which means it can continue to work at much greater heights. Nevertheless, it takes a massive amount of fuel to overcome the force of gravity and project the spacecraft into space.

Battle of the forces?

A moving vehicle is affected by several different forces, which push or pull it in different directions. Some forces act directly against each other, but the driver or rider uses these forces to control the vehicle. The next time you travel in a vehicle think about all the forces that are acting together at any one moment to start, move, steer or stop the vehicle.

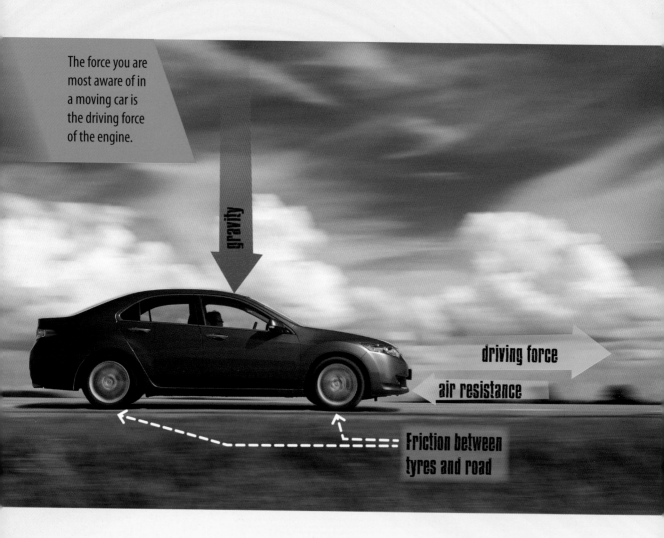

The force you are most aware of in a moving car is the driving force of the engine.

gravity

driving force

air resistance

Friction between tyres and road

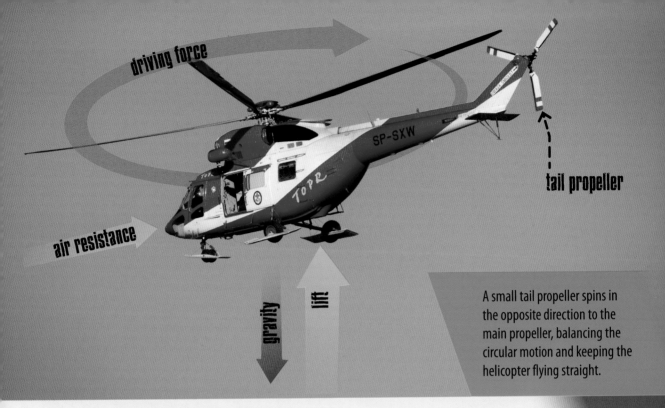

driving force

tail propeller

air resistance

gravity

lift

A small tail propeller spins in the opposite direction to the main propeller, balancing the circular motion and keeping the helicopter flying straight.

For and against movement

The driving force comes from the engine or from the rider's muscles. Ranged against it are friction, air resistance and, if the vehicle is a boat, water resistance. Friction both helps and hinders the driver. On the positive side, it provides braking force and allows a road vehicle to grip the road. On the negative side, it decreases the effect of the driving force.

Reducing the opposing forces

Vehicles that are built for speed are designed to reduce the negative effects of friction and air or water resistance. Smooth surfaces create less friction than rough ones, so designers use smooth surfaces. Streamlining reduces air and water resistance.

Forces that push up or pull down

Gravity is the main force pulling vehicles down. This is helpful when, for example, a bicycle goes over a bump and gravity pulls it back down to the ground. Friction is affected by gravity – the greater the gravity (or weight), the greater the force of friction. Two forces oppose gravity: upthrust allows boats to float in the water, and lift produced by aircraft wings and helicopter blades allows aircraft to fly.

1. A wheel makes movement easier because:
   a) it rolls
   b) it has a tyre
   c) as the hub makes a small circle, the rim makes a large circle
   d) it has spokes

2. Which of these is not true?
   a) friction allows you to push off against the ground on a scooter
   b) brakes use friction to work
   c) friction helps you to grip the handlebars
   d) friction makes the wheels spin faster

3. The chain on a bicycle:
   a) links the front wheel to the handlebars
   b) links the gear wheels to the front wheel
   c) links the pedals to the chain wheel
   d) links the chain wheel to the gear wheel

4. A penny-farthing takes more effort than a modern bicycle because:
   a) the back wheel is so small
   b) the rider can't touch the ground
   c) it has no pedals
   d) the front wheel is so large and it has no chain

5. How many gears does this bicycle have?
   a) three
   b) six
   c) nine
   d) seven

6 In a suspension bridge, the weight of the main cable is supported by:
  a) the roadway
  b) the towers and the anchorage points
  c) the towers
  d) the hangers, which join the cable to the roadway

7 Trains can travel faster than cars because:
  a) their wheels do not have treads
  b) they are powered by electricity
  c) the rails and wheels are smooth, so there is little friction
  d) they are bigger and heavier than cars

8 Which of these things is not true for a maglev train?
  a) it has no wheels
  b) it is slower than high-speed electric trains
  c) it floats above the track
  d) it is propelled by the force of magnetism

9 A boat floats when:
  a) the upthrust is greater than gravity
  b) the upthrust equals gravity
  c) the upthrust is less than gravity
  d) there is no upthrust

10 An aircraft wing has flaps that are lowered:
  a) to make the aircraft move faster
  b) to make the wing narrower
  c) to give the wing more uplift
  d) to save fuel

Glossary

air resistance force that slows down the movement of an object through the air

axle rod that connects the hubs of two or more wheels

buoyant able to float

cable thick wire made of many thinner strands twisted together

carbon dioxide gas that is produced when a once-living thing burns. Carbon dioxide is a greenhouse gas.

chain wheel toothed wheel that links the pedals of a bicycle to the chain

climate change extreme weather and changes to expected patterns of climates around the world produced by global warming

cog tooth on the rim of a wheel that fits between the teeth of another wheel or into the links of a chain

compressed squashed or squeezed by a force

crankshaft rod that changes the up-and-down movement of an engine into a circular movement

density weight of an object compared to its size

electromagnet magnet produced by electricity flowing through a coil of wire wound around an iron core

exhaust gases waste gases

flange lip attached to the rim of a train wheel to stop it sliding off a rail

friction force produced when one surface moves over another surface. Friction acts to slow down the movement.

gear toothed wheel that fits into a chain or other toothed wheel to change the speed of movement

gear wheel toothed wheel that links the chain of a bicycle to the hub of the back wheel

gravity force of attraction between two objects. On Earth, gravity pulls everything towards the ground. This is because Earth's mass is much greater than everything around it.

greenhouse gases gases that trap heat in the atmosphere and so make Earth warmer

hub centre of a wheel

internal combustion engine engine that burns petrol or other fuel inside the engine to move pistons up and down

lever simple machine that magnifies the effect of a force. A lever is a rod or pole that moves around a point to make something move.

lift force that lifts something up

magnetism forces produced by a magnet or magnets

oxygen gas that is needed for something to burn

piston part of an engine that moves up and down

pivot point around which a lever turns

pneumatic filled with compressed air

rudder device on a boat or ship below the surface of the water that is used for steering

skid slide out of control

span distance from one side to another

spokes thin, strong wire rods that join the hub of a wheel to the rim

streamlined shaped so that air or water moves easily around an object

suspension bridge type of bridge in which the road or rail track is hung from an overhead cable

tread moulded raised pattern on a tyre or sole of a shoe that increases grip between tyre or shoe and the ground

tyre rubber cover around the rim of a wheel

upthrust force that pushes up an object in a liquid

water resistance force that slows down the movement of an object through water

Find out more

Books

Forces and Motion (Mind Webs), Anna Claybourne (Wayland, 2014)

Forces and Motion (Hands-on Science), Jack Challoner and Maggie Hewson (Kingfisher, 2013)

Motorbikes (Ultimate Machines), Rob Scott Colson (Wayland, 2013)

Websites

www.bbc.co.uk/bitesize/ks2/science/physical_processes/forces/read/1
This BBC website gives basic information about forces. When you've read it, you can try a quiz.

www.physics4kids.com/files/motion_friction.html
Want to know more about friction? This website shows how friction affects cars and aircraft and how materials are measured for how much friction they generate.

www.sciencekids.co.nz/gamesactivities/forcesinaction.html
Play the game that compares how far a truck travels along a track when you increase the slope and the weight of its load. Try adding a parachute to the back of the truck.

Places to visit

Science Museum
Exhibition Road
South Kensington
London SW7 2DD
www.sciencemuseum.com

This is the world's largest science museum of its kind. It has 40 galleries that explore scientific breakthroughs and include hands-on exhibits.

Coventry Transport Museum
Millennium Place
Hales Street
Coventry CV1 1JD
www.transport-museum.com

This museum has the largest collection of British cars in the world. You can see ThrustSCC, the world's fastest car. You can also ride the simulator as this record-breaking car reaches 1,228 kilometres (763 miles) per hour – faster than the speed of sound.

National Rail Museum
Leeman Road
York YO26 4XJ
www.nrm.org.uk

This museum in York focuses on the railways and, including its locomotion collection at Shildon, has more than a million objects, such as locomotives, carriages and everything else used to build and run a railway.

Royal Air Force Museum
www.rafmuseum.org.uk

This incredible museum is on two sites, one in London and the other in Cosford in the Midlands. Between them, they have more than 170 aircraft arranged in themed halls with films, interactive displays and the history of flying.

Further research

- If you have a bicycle, examine it carefully to see for yourself how the brakes, pedals and gears work.

- The Tour de France is the most famous and most challenging cycle race in the world. Find out about the type of challenges it sets and how the race is organized. Many other races are held in particular places on certain dates. See if there is one near you that you can go and watch – or take part in!

- There are many museums featuring different types of transport in different parts of the country. Find out which are closest to you and try to visit one or more. If the museum has earlier forms of vehicle, find out what has changed over time to make the vehicle faster. Does it have a bigger engine? Is it more streamlined?

- Think about how transport might develop in the future. Find out about new types of engine, such as hybrids (cars that have both a petrol and an electric engine) and vehicles that run on hydrogen fuel cells.

Index